Autumn Harvest

How to Harvest the Value Within Your Small Business

Michael Ringler, CPA

Autumn Harvest

Printed by:
CreateSpace Independent
Publishing Platform

Copyright © 2017, Michael Ringler

Published in the United States of America

ISBN-13: 978-1976426575
ISBN-10: 197642657X

No parts of this publication may be reproduced without correct attribution
to the author of this book.

**This publication is meant to introduce and broaden your knowledge. It is not
a substitute for the advice of your accountant, attorney or any other advisors,
personal or professional..**

Here's What's Inside...

Introduction..1

Why Don't More Business Owners Know How to Harvest the Value of Their Businesses? 3

The Importance of Having an Exit Plan in Place Before a Triggering Event 6

Your Professional Team 10

Valuation Methods 14

Formalizing Your Buy/Sell Stock Redemption.. 18

Tax Aspects of a Sale 20

How One Company Got it Wrong and It Cost them Their Business 21

How to Harvest the Value Within Your Small Business.. 23

Introduction

Autumn Harvest!

Many entrepreneurs' have the bulk of their financial net worth invested in their closely held business. They've invested a significant portion of their lives building and nurturing the business but haven't yet designed an exit plan; an exit plan to determine how to harvest the value within their business.

It is important to take the time to complete the following key components to harvesting value:

1. Decide the exit plan is important
2. Coordinate your team
3. Execute and implement the plan.

Once complete, the plan is in motion so that when you have a triggering event - a sale, death or disability - you are in a position to harvest the value of your business and not scrambling after the fact. In this book I'm going to walk you through the different facets of an Exit Plan so you can see that it's not as difficult or ponderous as you may have thought.

I hope this book inspires you to place significant value on the development of your Exit Plan so that when you are ready, you and your family may harvest the value in the autumn of your life.

To Your Continued Success!

Michael Ringler, CPA

Why Don't More Business Owners Know How to Harvest the Value of Their Businesses?

Susan: Good afternoon. This is Susan Austin. I am super excited to be here with Mike Ringler, who is going to share his thoughts and ideas on how to harvest the value within your small business. Welcome, Michael.

Michael: Thanks, Susan. I look forward to chatting.

Susan: Me as well. Why don't more business owners already know how to harvest the value of their businesses, Mike?

Michael: Most small business owners know upfront that, at some point in time, they're going to need to find an appropriate value for their business, so they can take it to market and get an appropriate price for the value they've built over many years, even over the course of their career. The value of a closely held/privately held business is really one large component of a family's net worth, just like any other type of a bank account, certificate of deposit, or mutual fund. The investment in their business often represents significant wealth, and, often, during those wealth-building years, while they're working hard to grow the business they are forfeiting other opportunities to make suitable investments. A lot of times, this becomes their most significant asset and one that needs to be harvested at some point for a lot of different reasons, one of which could be maintaining a specific lifestyle in retirement. It could also fuel other investments by diversifying the cash proceeds after the sale, or it could be used for philanthropy. Many entrepreneurs have good intentions to help their communities, and their companies represent real wealth that needs to be nurtured and managed. Then, at the end, it needs to be realized.

Another reason many entrepreneurs don't know how to harvest the value of their businesses is that they don't begin with the end in mind. Instead, they begin with the beginning in mind, meaning the business is formed around just a single product or service, and all of the entrepreneur's energy goes into marketing that product or service.

At that stage, it's a simple model. It's only later, as the business grows, that other complexities seem to slip in. Those other complexities could be hiring new team members, technology, marketing, or banking. Each and every one really distracts the entrepreneur from thinking about what they're going to do with the business down the road.

Pretty soon, the years just peel off the calendar, and they've built a business of some value, but they don't know how to harvest that value. It's not part of their expertise, it's not something they have experience with, and it's not urgent enough to make it to the top of the to-do list.

Then the problem becomes that it never gets done. There are horror stories associated with not having a plan in place. Once a death or disability occurs, it's relatively too late to get a fair or true value for a business. The good news is, there have been some very successful stories of entrepreneurs and their families putting this type of a structure in place because they carved out the time for it and made it a priority.

I've seen it work really well when the owner is in good health, and they're ready to retire. They get a premium price for their business. I've also seen it work with great success when there has been an unexpected death or disability. It is essential to have the mechanism or structure in place for how to value the business, how to sell the business, and how to get fairly compensated for the value that the owner put into the business, so that their family is protected.

The Importance of Having an Exit Plan in Place Before a Triggering Event

Susan: That is a perfect segue because I wanted to ask you, what the impact would be on a business owner who doesn't take the time to put a plan in place?

Michael: For most business owners and their families, having an exit plan in place is going to require creating a vision for what they want to happen and then setting goals and objectives for the things that are important to the family. Some of those goals and objectives could be securing a certain income in retirement, taking a long-put-off dream vacation, funding children or grandchildren's educations, or donating to charity. This is exciting for the business owner because, often, all of their money has been tied up in their business, and they have had to put off doing these things. Having a proper exit plan in place allows them to do all the things they've always wanted to do.

Let me give you an example from August 2016. We met with a business owner who was 60 years old and appeared to be in great health, but while working on the family cottage, had a massive heart attack and died.

Fortunately, he had other partners in the business, so its success was not conditioned on him being the only value driver.

His wife and family, however, through their grieving process, were very concerned about what his passing would mean for them financially. The company had had the foresight to sit down with their trusted advisors five to ten years before and put together a plan in the case of a death or disability that would fairly compensate the family of the person who passed or became disabled. Because of this, we could execute according to the plan, with minimal challenges, and were able to secure the value of the business for the family without any economic hardship to the remaining business owners. We had a structure and a system in place. In this case, it was funded through a life insurance policy. Relatively small insurance premiums had been paid over the last 10 years, but they had a significant impact when this business owner passed.

That's probably the best example I can recall recently of an entrepreneurial family having the foresight to get it done when they didn't need to get it done. In that horrific moment when somebody unexpectedly passed, they had the system and the process in place to value the business, redeem the shareholders' interest, and compensate the family for their loved one's value. Because of that, the family was able to do a lot of things they otherwise would not have been able to do, and they didn't put a big burden on the company.

Susan: So many business owners put their entire lives into their companies. To not be able to get the full value and provide for their families or do charity endeavors or whatever they want to at this stage of their lives seems like such a shame, such a mistake.

Michael: It really is. There are a couple of options when that happens. The company might have to go through liquidation. If there was not a structure in place, there could be all types of problems, including differences of opinion in how the business should be valued. That was not an issue in this situation because it was spelled out in the redemption agreement.

Another issue could be the fact that funding the buyout of a deceased owner can be a significant strain and hardship on the remaining owners and the business. This was not the case in the situation I described because they had a funding mechanism—namely insurance—in place. Therefore, the insurance proceeds were payable to the company as the beneficiary, so the money came into the business and then went right back out to the deceased owner's spouse for the redemption of the stock.

From the company's perspective, it was cash in, cash out, but there can be trouble when there is not a mechanism in place with insurance. In this case, the company or the remaining stockholders have to come up with the value of the business out-of-pocket.

This can put them in a very difficult place because suddenly the company has debt. If they must go to the bank or if they have to finance the purchase over time, they've purchased a shareholder's interest, which is really unfortunate because it is a non-performing asset. It's one thing to finance a long-term asset like equipment or real estate, but an asset like the redemption of a stock in a privately held company becomes a non-performing asset. The objective, in this case, becomes to finance any future buyout with life insurance, so the company is not harmed from a cash flow perspective.

Your Professional Team

Susan: Let's switch gears and talk about what business owners need to know, so they can harvest the value of their businesses when the time comes.

Michael: It starts with developing a team while keeping three components in mind. First, the business owner needs a top-notch attorney who can think through and draft the underlying documents that become the stock redemption agreement. Then, of course, they need the help of a qualified CPA (certified public accountant) to assist them in structuring the transaction and the tax impacts of the transaction. Lastly, they need the help of an insurance agent.

The CPA helps determine an appropriate method to value the business. There are a multitude of recognizable valuation methods. It's the CPA's responsibility to take a look at the type of industry the business is in; take a look at the financial metrics of the business; and work with the management team to determine any risks associated with the business on a go-forward basis, as well as any plans they have for growth. The answers to those questions will lead the CPA to the most appropriate method to value the business.

I've seen situations where the CPA is not involved in the valuation, but the business owners are. By the time either the death has occurred or the owners are ready to sell the business, the valuations that the management team put together are so far off of a fair value that, especially in the event of death, it becomes a contentious issue because the management team had an idea of what the value is, but that isn't necessarily fair value at the present time. Inevitably, each side—the business side and the shareholder's estates—retain separate legal counsel, and it becomes a struggle to agree on what the true price should be.

That's why it's important to have a CPA involved on the front end; they not only identify the proper valuation methodology but also build out a valuation that makes sense and is fair to all parties. There are designations relative to certified business valuation experts, but although that's preferred, it's not necessary. In my opinion, as long as the CPA is well-versed in valuation methodologies, they can come up with a valuation that makes sense for that business.

Susan: Does the CPA need to have a history with that company? Is it better to use someone who knows the business inside out, or are fresh, objective eyes better?

Michael: CPA firms may or may not have that capability within their practices. If they do, then it absolutely makes sense for a business to use them because they have history with the company and know the industry. They've seen the company through good times and not-so-good times, and they're a trusted advisor to all parties at that point. If a CPA is well-versed in valuation methods, they should do the valuation.

If the business's CPA firm is smaller and doesn't have that capability, it's very important for the ownership group to search for a firm that has that capability and expertise.

Susan: Who else do they need on their team?

Michael: The attorney is critical for drafting up documents. Typically, there are provisions in the document that explain who, what, and how. *Who* refers to the interested parties; *what* refers to what happens upon death, disability, or the sale of the business; and *how* identifies the method and the structure of the redemption. The redemption agreement—the *how* part—could entail the valuation method agreed upon; it could discuss the payment terms.

The attorney needs to be versed and experienced in transactional law and small business matters because the business needs an agreement that can hold up in court, if needed; that has a reasonable basis for support; and that's fair to all parties.

Finally, the business needs an insurance agent who can put the funding mechanism in place. The business owners own 100% of the stock, so they're the ones who will eventually sell the business or will need to buy out a partner if there is a death or disability. This is a critical part of the process for the owners.

Valuation Methods

Susan: How can they go about putting together a good valuation for the business? What does that process look like?

Michael: Once there has been a decision to prepare a business valuation, it's the CPA's role to look for the most appropriate method to value that specific business. Typically, there are four recognizable methods for valuing a business.

The first method, which is the simplest method, is called "book value." The book value method involves taking a snapshot of the company's balance sheet at a specific point in time and identifying what is the stockholder's equity. By definition, stockholder's equity is the difference between the total assets of the company and the total liabilities of the company. The total assets include cash, receivables, inventory, and fixed assets. The liabilities—the amounts owed to other people—are deducted from the total assets.. The amount leftover represents the stockholder's equity. While book value is the simplest way to value a business, oftentimes it's not the most accurate.

The second valuation method is called the "going concern" method. The going concern method is usually used in situations where a company is not doing well.

Perhaps they've experienced significant losses or changes in management. Perhaps they've lost a key customer or a key supplier, or the bank won't finance them anymore. In that situation, the going concern method will take a look at the assets and try to determine a liquidation value as if the company were going out of business. In a lot of cases, the value will be a lot less than even the book value. The going concern method is really appropriate for troubled businesses, and the reason the value is less is the owners are under a significant amount of duress at that point, and they're willing to not realize full value on their assets, so they can get out of the mess.

The third method is a very popular method called "the capitalized returns method." It takes a historical look at the earnings of the business, typically over a three- to seven-year period, and normalizes those earnings for items that would not recur or for items that are excessive in nature, such as rent expenses, officer compensation, and vehicle expenses. In effect, those types of expenses are added back to the net earnings to get normalized earnings. A capitalization rate is applied to those normalized earnings. The capitalization rate is a rate at which an investor would be willing to make an investment and get a certain rate of return from that investment.

For example, if a company had normalized earnings of $100,000 with a capitalization rate of 20%, it would take the $100,000 of earnings and divide by the 20% to determine the value of that business to be $500,000.

This method is very different than book value and going concern. The capitalized returns method is typically for healthy, stable companies that have mature earning streams.

The fourth and final valuation method is the "discounted future earnings" method. This is appropriate when a company is coming out of startup mode, where perhaps they haven't had earnings because they've been reinvesting in the business. They're at a point where they believe that the significant investments are behind them and that future earnings are going to be significant and eventually stabilize.

This method requires a projection of what those earnings could look like over a five- to seven-year period. Once those earnings are calculated, they are discounted back to present value, and a capitalization rate is applied to them. The resulting value is the net earnings over that period of time discounted back to the present value and divided by the capitalization rate.

Susan: How do you determine the best valuation method for a particular business?

Michael: I determine it with a combination of professional experience and expertise in valuation methods. I have a matrix for a company's financial characteristics. It's a square with four squares inside of it. Depending on the company's characteristics, it will lend itself to being in the box for book value, being in the box for going concern, being in the box for discounted future earnings, or being in the box for capitalized returns.

If an inexperienced person tried to value a company, they might pick an appropriate valuation methodology, but it might not be appropriate for the company's specific situation. For example, they may pick book value for a value of $200,000, but if the capitalized returns method was used, it would have been $500,000. In that simple example, the company would have left $300,000 on the table.

Formalizing Your Buy/Sell Stock Redemption

Susan: Talk to us about formalizing the buy/sell stock redemption.

Michael: Formalizing the buy/sell agreement, otherwise known as a stock redemption agreement, is critically important to protect all parties in the event of a future sale or the death or disability of a stockholder. It provides proof of agreement at a specific point in time, and it provides the mechanics through which the business valuation will be prepared and how the buyout will be structured. It also may indicate that a valuation needs to be prepared in reasonable time intervals—typically every three to five years—to update the value of the business as well as to make sure that the funding mechanism—especially life insurance—is adequate for the purchase price period.

For example, if in the year 2010, a valuation had been prepared resulting in a value of $1 million, at that point in time, the shareholders would have gone to the marketplace and obtained a life insurance policy with a face value of $1 million.

Five years later, if the company has now grown in value from $1 million to $2 million, but the shareholders are not aware of this or an updated valuation has not been prepared to evidence this increase, then the business owners may be uninsured in the case of a death or disability, leaving an exposure of $1 million. Therefore, it's critical in regular intervals to update the valuation and to ensure appropriate life insurance is in force for the value of the business.

Tax Aspects of a Sale

Susan: How are taxes handled when it comes to the sale of a business?

Michael: The tax aspects of a sale of a business are typically handled in one of two ways.

One way is a stock sale whereby the business owner sells their stock to the purchaser. This method has a positive impact on the seller of the stock because the sales proceeds or profits are taxed at the lower capital gains rate. In this situation, the seller benefits from a larger net proceed after the taxes have been paid.

The second method is an asset sale, where the specific assets of the business are sold to a buyer. This reduces the net proceeds to the seller because the tax rates on the sale of assets are generally higher than the sale of stock.

In addition, if there are any distributions to the shareholder once those corporate assets have been sold, that distribution may also be taxed at the personal level. The preferred method for a seller is a stock sale.

How One Company Got it Wrong, and It Cost them Their Business

Susan: Can you share some more examples of people you've helped?

Michael: I worked with two owners of a business. One of the owners wanted out, and the other owner wanted him out. Collectively, they decided on the purchase price for the stock without consulting a professional service provider to properly prepare a valuation. Unfortunately, the valuation they came up with was significantly higher than what the true value of the business was, and because the company was redeeming the stock of the departing shareholder, their valuation saddled the company with significant debt. Eventually, it could not afford the debt and was forced into liquidation.

If a valuation had been performed, I'm certain the dollar amount would have been significantly less than what was agreed to, and that would have predicated a smaller payment from the company, which redeemed the stock to the shareholder. Doing this could have saved the company money because they had other debts—namely bank debt, and by paying the former shareholder large amounts that really created no value, they didn't have enough to pay the bank in a timely fashion.

The bank came in and demanded their loans, and, as a result, they had to shut down the business.

A similar analogy: A person and their friend own a business together. The friend wants to sell their coffee mug to the other owner, and the other owner wants to buy it because they don't want their friend to drink coffee anymore. The owners agree that the buyer will pay $20 for the mug, but the mug is only worth $2. The owner overpays by $18. Any other person would have said, "That cup is worth $2, not $20," but now the owner is required to pay their friend $20 because that's what they agreed on. Unfortunately, the owner can't afford to make the payments.

In the real case, the owners didn't know better. We were referred to do some accounting work, so we started looking at the assets and the liabilities and we asked about the big promissory note to Susan. Dave had bought Susan's stock and paid $600,000 for it. I estimated the stock was actually worth about $200,000. In the meantime, payments of an extra $400,000 were being made for the client. It totally drained all the cash out of the business, and they couldn't pay their people, their rent, or their line of credit with the bank. The bank wasn't happy and forced them into liquidation. .

How to Harvest the Value Within Your Small Business

Susan: I can see that. If someone is interested in working with you, how far in advance should they prepare? And what's the process you take them through?

Michael: The proper time to start exit planning is when a company has been in business for about three years. I don't think that's too early to start contemplating and putting some pieces in place. By year three, they have already been through the startup phase, so they're beginning to become profitable and generating some value. That's when they need to put some mechanisms in place to protect them. Around that three-year mark, they should start assembling their team, if they don't have one already, and start having conversations about preparing a business valuation and a redemption agreement.

We take our clients through our five-step Business Valuation Foundation Process. The first step is the Discovery Process, the second step is the Critical Factors Analysis, the third step is the Valuation Breakthrough, the fourth step is the Creation Process, and the fifth step is the Grand Huddle.

Once this process is completed, the business ownership is benefited by having a valuation in place that supports a buy/sell agreement, an estate plan, or any gifting strategies.

If someone has questions, they can call us at **586-954-2990** or shoot me an email at **mringler@ringlercpa.com**.

Susan: Thank you, Mike, for walking us through this. I can see where trying to do this alone and not having the right team in place could open a business up to big problems.

Michael: You are welcome, Susan. It really isn't something a business should put off. As I said earlier, once a business is established and out of their startup phase, they ought to put an exit strategy in place to protect what they are building.

Here's How to Harvest the Value within Your Small Business....

Your business has value. A critical strategy is orchestrating a process to ensure that you receive fair value for your investment in your business. This will arise when you are ready to sell or you experience a death or disability within the ownership ranks.

That's where we come in. We help business owners just like you harvest the value of your small business by maximizing an exit strategy that can withstand an uncertain future.
If you are a business owner with:

1. Revenue > $1,000,000
2. 10 – 100 employees
3. Profits > 5% of sales
4. Then,

Step 1: Call us at **586.954.2990** or email **mringler@ringlercpa.com** to schedule a free, 30-minute discovery call to further understand the benefits of an Exit Plan.

Step 2: We will talk you through our Business Valuation Foundation Program, identifying the necessary steps to arrive at an appropriate valuation method for your business.

Step 3: From there, we will utilize our Attorney Match Program to allow for the creation of the buy/sell and redemption agreements.

Step 4: We will repeat the valuation every three to five years to capture any necessary changes to the plan.

Many business owners put off developing their exit strategy because they're inundated with the day-to-day operations of their business and have not placed a priority on this critical planning, but not you.

Now with our help you can harvest the value of your business by creating an exit plan that will protect and enhance your family's financial future. Whether it is a sale, death or disability, we have the tools, processes and expertise to assist you realize the value of your of business in the autumn of your life.

To get started, send us an email to: **mringler@ringlercpa.com** and we'll take it from there.

About the Author

Michael Ringler, CPA, is an advisor to business owners in the areas of tax, valuations and family wealth. Mike is a graduate of Michigan State University, earning a Bachelor of Arts in Accounting in 1984.

In 1992, he formed Ringler CPA, a boutique accounting firm assisting entrepreneurial families.

The Company website is at **www.ringlercpa.com**.

www.ingramcontent.com/pod-product-compliance
Lightning Source LLC
Chambersburg PA
CBHW050034230526
45470CB00003B/1264